| 이향아 영역 시집 |

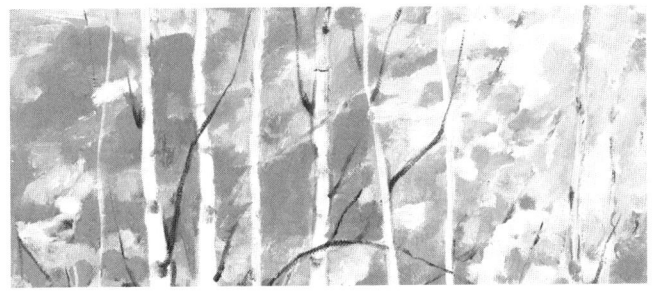

# 저녁 강가에서
### By The Riverside At Eventide

by HyangAh Lee
Trans. by JohngHo Lee

창조문예사

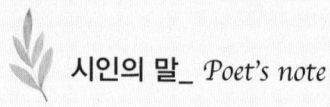
## 시인의 말_ *Poet's note*

### 한 생애의 하루

오늘은 한 생애의 하루.
아침에 눈을 뜰 때면, 내 한 생애 가운데 가장 아름다운 날로 살게 해 달라고 기도합니다.

저녁 강가에서 흐르는 물을 바라보면, 마음도 물결처럼 잔잔하게 흐릅니다.
저녁 강가에서 먼 하늘을 바라보면 그리운 사람들의 얼굴이 떠오릅니다.
저녁 강가에 서면 세상이 웅장한 교회당처럼 나를 감싸서, 내 하루의 욕망이 얼마나 부질없는 것이었는지 깨닫게 합니다.
뜨겁던 하루는 끝나고, 나도 이제는 집으로 돌아가야 한다는 것을 알게 됩니다.

오늘 한영대조시집 『저녁 강가에서』의 원고를 마무리하여 마음이 가볍습니다. 그러나 한편으로는 내게 과분하고 사치스러운 일이 아닌가 하는 생각도 듭니다.

## One Day Among My Lifetime

Today is one day among my lifetime.

When I open my eyes in the morning, I always pray I could live today as the best time in my lifetime.

When I gaze upon the waves by the riverside at eventide, I feel my mind is flowing quietly like the water.

When I look up at the sky afar by the riverside at eventide, there are emerging the faces I've longed for.

When I'm on the riverside at eventide, the whole world covers up me as if it is a grand chapel, and awakens me how my earthly desire of a day is in vain.

The sun, the heat of a day, is ready to set down slowly. And now I get to know I've to go home also.

I am very happy with a light heart that I have finished today my manuscript of contrastive poems of Korean-English, 「By The Riverside At Eventide」. It is supposed

이것은 우연히 어쩌다가 된 일이 아니며, 특별한 일이기 때문입니다. 보이지 않는 손이 나를 붙잡아 여기까지 왔습니다.

먼저 번역해 주신 이정호 선생님께 감사합니다.
이정호 선생님은 유럽 각국의 신앙시와 영국 낭만주의 시대의 거장인 로버트 번스, 윌리엄 워즈워스, 새뮤얼 콜리지, 로드 바이런, 셸리, 키츠 등의 시들을 많이 번역하셨습니다. 이향아의 시에 토착어를 비롯하여 궁벽한 어휘들이 많은데도, 여러 번 음미하고 세밀하게 대조하면서 수고를 아끼지 않으셨습니다.
시의 어휘가 얼마나 오묘하고 다채로운 광채로 분화하는가를, 어느 시인보다도 명확히 알고 계시는 선생님, 진실로 누구보다도 시를 사랑하시는 선생님께 경의를 표합니다.
이 시집 출간을 위해서 오래 마음을 써 주신 월간 『창조문예』 발행인 임만호 선생님께 깊은 감사를 드립니다. 선생님께서는 어려운 여건을 개의치 않으시고 여러 해 동안 『창조

too much luxurious for me.

It is not ordinary, but very special one. The invisible hands have led me to be here.

First of all, I would like to send my thanks to Mr JohngHo Lee.

He had translated into Korean many spiritual poems of European countries, and English Romantic Poems by Robert Burns, William Wordsworth, Samuel T. Coleridge, Lord Byron, Percy B. Shelley, John Keats, etc. He has translated also the works of HyangAh Lee, though she used to compose her poems using Korean native and secluded idioms.

I am sure he surely has good understandings on the spectrums of colorfully occult vocabulary, better than the other poets. I would like to show my respects to him who loves poems.

문예』지면을 할애하여 영역된 이향아의 시를 연재해 주셨습니다. 베풀어 주신 따뜻한 보살핌을 잊지 않겠습니다. 그리고 감사하는 마음으로 정진하겠습니다.

2020년 5월 연지당硯池堂에서 이향아

And also I wish to thank Mr ManHo Lim, the publisher of 『The Monthly Changjomunyae』, who is thoughtful for my anthology and serialized my poems translated into English, and I'll remember his warm regards. I'll devote myself to create good literary works.

HyangAh Lee<br>
from YounGyDang<br>
May 2020

 **옮긴이의 말_** *Translator's note*

# 시인의 의도에 밀착된 또 하나의 작품

시를 번역하려고 할 때, 시인에게 알고 싶은 중요한 사항이 있습니다. 시작詩作 당시 그 소재에 대한 시인의 느낌과 정서는 어떠했고, 왜 그 시어를 선택했으며, 메타포는 무엇인가 하는 것입니다. 이런 내용을 미루어 짐작하여 번역하면 오역의 가능성이 커지기 때문입니다.

그동안 이향아 시인을 직접 만나 배경 설명을 듣고 상의한 것이 수없이 많았습니다. 가능한 한 시인의 의도에 밀착된 또 하나의 작품을 만들려는 노력을 십분 이해했으리라 믿습니다.

그런 후에 나의 일천한 영어 실력으로 적합한 시어를 찾아내서 한 편의 영시가 되도록 꾸려야 했는데, 이것이 내게는 버거운 작업이었습니다.

단언컨대 이향아 시인의 시는 정말 아름답고 매력적입니다. 시의적절하게 사용된 시어들, 토속적인 아름다운 말들, 반전의 반전을 이루는 구성들, 무엇 하나 만만한 대목이 없었습니다. 포기하고 싶은 마음이 들 때도 있었음을 고백합니다. 그럴 때마다 격려해 준 친지들과 창조문예 대표 임만

## Another Poems To Match With The Original Ones

To traslate poems I always wish to understand what the poet feels from the subject material, why the composer selects those poetic vocabulary, and what the metaphor of it is. If I happen to translate some works as my feeling leads without those understandings, it should be fallen into the mistranslations.

During that time I have met the poet, Professor HyangAh Lee, so many times and listen to her on the above questions. I believe she could understand my effort sufficiently to produce a work to match with her poem.

After that, to extract a suitable words from my short knowledges and compose a new poems in English is too big works for me.

I affirm without hesitation in saying that her poems are very beautifully woven with proper, native, even gorgeous poetic vocabulary, and their constitutions reversed after reversals, that is, nothing is easy. Herewith I confess that

호 장로의 우격다짐식 권면에 결국은 원고를 다 넘기는 작업을 마치게 되었습니다. 찬찬히 교정봐 준 출판사 직원분들께 고마움을 전합니다.
   그리고 지금까지 인도하여 주신 하나님께 감사드립니다.

이정호

once I wished to give up its translation, but by encouraging almost high-handed from friends, especially, ManHo Lim, the publisher of 『The Monthly Changjomunyae』, I have come to complete the manuscript. Also I have to thank proofreaders in the company for their careful works.

And most of all, I thank God for the grace bestowed upon me to finish this translation works.

JohngHo Lee

# 차례

시인의 말_ *Poet's note* — 2

옮긴이의 말_ *Translator's note* — 8

## 제1부_ 봄 바다 파도처럼

꽃다발을 말리며_ Drying Flowers — 18

아지랑이처럼 살아요_ Like A Haze Am I Leading My Life — 22

적막을 위하여_ An Ode To The Solitude — 24

저 새들 좀 봐_ Look, Those Birds — 26

봄 바다 파도처럼_ Like The Waves In Spring — 28

씨앗 속에는_ In A Seed — 30

저녁 메밀밭_ The Buckwheat Field In The Twilight — 32

해바라기_ The Sunflower — 34

꽃차를 마시며_ Teaing The Flower Tea — 36

여름 산을 바라보고 있으면
　_ When I Look At The Summer Mountain — 38

풀꽃_ The Weed Flower — 40

깊은 잠_ Sound Slumber — 44

## 제2부_ 세상의 후미진 곳에서

| | |
|---|---|
| 안부_ Warm Regards | 48 |
| 유서를 쓰던 밤_ The Night When I Wrote A Will | 52 |
| 찻잔의 모서리에_ On the Rim Of A Cup | 54 |
| 아름다운 목소리로 후회하고 싶었다 _ I Wished To Repent Myself With A Sweet Voice | 57 |
| 봄밤_ Spring Night | 58 |
| 꽃_ The Flower | 62 |
| 저녁 강가에서_ By The Riverside At Eventide | 66 |
| 연연_ Lingering Affections | 70 |
| 세상의 후미진 곳에서_ At The Deeply Secluded Place | 72 |
| 나는 지금 다시_ I'm Going To Fall Asleep Again | 74 |
| 내 가슴 등잔에 불을 댕겨서 _ By Kindling A Lantern In My Heart | 76 |
| 날궂이_ The Foul Day | 78 |
| 어디 갔을까_ I Wonder Where You'd Gone | 80 |

## 제3부_ 아침에는 이슬이

| | |
|---|---|
| 문패_ The Name Plate | 84 |
| 편지_ A Letter | 86 |
| 어머니의 밥_ The Meals Of Mom | 88 |
| 동행_ Companion | 92 |
| 내 가슴의 고요_ The Serenity Of My Heart | 94 |
| 빨래를 널고서_ I Hung Out The Washes | 98 |
| 아침에는 이슬이_ The Dewdrops In The Morn | 102 |
| 저녁 산_ The Even Mount | 104 |
| 집으로 간다_ I'm Going Home | 108 |
| 자족하기_ To Be Self-sufficient | 110 |
| 진실하게 말하려면 눈물이 나온다 _ I Am Tearing Whenever I'd Say Honestly | 112 |
| 오래된 얼굴_ Faces Of Long Familiar | 114 |
| 이후로도 우리를_ Even Since Then For Us | 116 |

## 제4부_ 경청하소서

| | |
|---|---|
| 해 넘어가기 전_ Before Sunset | 122 |
| 쪽빛 종말을 생각하며 | 124 |
| _ Thinking About The Indigo Blue End Of The World | |
| 당신의 피리_ Your Flute | 126 |
| 소돔의 여자_ A Woman Of Sodom | 130 |
| 어쩌다 나 같은 것이_ How I, A Wretched | 132 |
| 돌아다보리_ Yet, I Would Look Back | 136 |
| 새 동아줄_ A New Rope | 140 |
| 좀 더 어리석게_ A Little More Foolish | 142 |
| 언제쯤 나는_ When Can I…… | 146 |
| 왕이신 당신_ You, My Lord | 148 |
| 우리가 사랑할 수 있다면_ If We Are Able To Love | 150 |
| 경청하소서_ May You Listen Close To Me | 154 |

# 제1부
## 봄 바다 파도처럼

*part* 1
## Like The Waves In Spring

## 꽃다발을 말리며

누가 내게
이와 같은 슬픔까지 알게 하는가
꽃이 피는 아픔도 예사가 아니거늘
저 순일한 목숨의 송이송이
붉은 울음을 꺾어다가
하필이면 내 손에서 시들게 하는가

예수가 십자가에 매달린 것처럼
꽃은 매달려서 절정을 모으고
영원히 사는 길을 맨발로 걸어서
이렇게 순하게 못 박히나니
다만 죽어서야
온전히 내게로 돌아오는 꽃이여
너를 안아 올리기에는
내 손이 너무 검게
너무 흉하게 여위었구나

황홀한 순간의 갈채는 지나가고
이제 남은 것은 빈혈의 꽃과
무심한 벽과
굳게 다문 우리들의 천 마디 말뿐

## Drying Flowers

Who on earth are you,
Making me feel such a sadness?
It's not usual for a flower to labor with bloom,
Furthermore, that pure lives of each blossom,
Their crimson weepings, dare you to pick
And become withered in my hand of all hands.

As Jesus crucified on the cross
The flower is reaching its summit by dangling,
Walking on an eternal way barefoot
Thus, crucified so obediently.
You are the flower, only by dying,
Returning wholly to my bossom.
To embrace and raise you up,
My hands are so much darkened
And awfully gaunt.

The ecstasy moment of applause has gone.
Now the remainders are the withered flower,
The heartless wall,
A thousand words of our dummy mouth shut,

아무것도 없다

죽어 가는 꽃을 거꾸로 매다노라면
물구나무서서 솟구치는
내 피의 열기
내 피의 노여움
내 피의 통곡

꽃을 말린다, 입술을 깨물고
검게 탄 내 피를 허공에 바랜다

Nothing else remains.

When I hang up the flowers dying,
The fever of my blood
Which is surging upside down,
The anger of my blood,
The wailing of my blood.

I'm drying the flowers, biting my lips.
I'm fading my tanned blood in the air.

## 아지랑이처럼 살아요

그래도 가끔은 내 생각도 하면서
더러는 이 근처를 지나기도 하겠지요
달빛으로 헹궈서 가라앉은 웃음으로
아지랑이처럼 살아요, 나는
예전의 불길은 고운 재로 덮어서
예전의 원망은 물살에 흘려
아지랑이처럼 가물거려요
아지랑이처럼 끄덕거려요
세월이란 무서워요
세월 덕분이지요
아지랑이처럼
아지랑이처럼
내가 살아요

# Like A Haze Am I Leading My Life

Yet, sometimes thinking about me
You may pass by this neighborhood.
With a calmed smile rinsed with the moonlight,
Like a haze am I leading my life.
As burying the old flames under the soft ashes,
Flowed down an old grudge on the stream of life,
They are only flickering like a haze,
And nodding like a haze.
Time is an awful thing.
It's a favor of time and tide.
Like a haze,
Like a haze,
I'm leading my life.

## 적막을 위하여

나는 그래도 호사스러운 편이다
이만큼 자주 적막할 수 있는 것은
이만큼 자주 적막하다고
일을 삼아 적막을 노래할 수 있는 것은

어제보다 낮아진 먼 산의 키를 재며
나는 아무런 불평도 없이
내 그림자 내가 밟고 홀로 서 있다
나는 바로 지금 적막한가 보다

이 적막함이여, 참으로 외람되다
이 적막함이여, 미안하다, 미안하다

약을 달이듯 흰 물을 끓인다
물은 아득한 시원의 적막으로부터 와서
나를 물들이겠지

내 적막은 이대로 눈부시겠지
모처럼 나를 위해 슬퍼해도 되겠지
화려하여라, 화려하여라
눈물이 나겠지

# An Ode To The Solitude

It belongs rather to luxury
That I'm solitary this much, so often,
Singing of solitude again and again
That I'm solitary.

Taking height of the mountain yonder, lowered recently
I, without any complaint,
Stood alone on my shadow.
It seems I am solitary in this moment.

Oh solitude, I'm presumptuous.
Oh solitude, I'm regretful, so regretful!

I'm boiling pure water as if decocting herbs.
The water has come from the solitude in the Beginning
And will dye me.

My solitude may be splendid itself.
It may be allowed for me to feel sorrow now.
Splendrous, what's more splendid!
Tears may be lingering in my eyes.

## 저 새들 좀 봐

줄지어 날아가는 저 기러기 좀 봐
금강하구 개펄에서
노을 깔린 하늘에서
수천수만이 일시에 춤을 추는
저 가창오리 떼 좀 봐

저 새들 좀 봐
흐르다가 잠기다가 일시에 솟구치는 것 좀 봐
깃털에서 깃털로 빛보다 빠른 선회
죽지를 틀어
오던 길을 버리고 되돌아갈 때도
누구 하나 슬프거나 섭섭하지 않게
세상 어느 귀퉁이도 구겨지지 않는다
천둥과 벼락이
오늘 밤 둥지를 덮칠지라도
새들은 길을 알아 두렵지 않다

## Look, Those Birds

Look, a flock of wild geese flying their ways in line.
At the lagoon along the estuary of the Kum River,
At the sky aglow with setting sun,
Look, those flock of the sute.
More than thousands of them are dancing all at once.

Look, those birds.
Look, they are floating, sinking, and raising up into air,
From feathers to feathers, whirling faster than the light.
Even when they are twisting their wings
And shifting the ways back and forth, so swiftly,
None of them would be grieved or sorry.
Any corner on the earth would not wrinkle.
Even though roars of thunder and lightning strikes
Their nests tonight,
The birds do not fear, for they know their daily living.

## 봄 바다 파도처럼

지금 생각하면 그럴 일도 아니건만
내가 그때 왜 그랬나 알 수가 없다
평생을 의지하며 살자던 그 말이
등짐 나눠 지고서 함께 가잔 그 말이
하도 붉어서
하도 진해서
좁은 어깨 오그려서 얼굴을 파묻고
봄 바다 파도처럼 흐느끼며 울었다
그대로 가라앉아 없어지고 싶었다
내가 그때 어리석게 울지만 않았어도
세상은 전혀 딴판이 되었을 걸
내가 그때 왜 그랬나 까닭을 모르겠다

# Like The Waves In Spring

Now I think it should not be done so.
I do not understand why I behaved so at that time.
His word to go through our lives relying on together,
To carry the burden of life together on our backs,
It was ever so red,
It was ever so deep.
I buried my face in my knees with shoulders shrunken,
And sobbed like the sea waves in spring,
Wishing to be sunken down, so melted away.
At that time if I did not sob sillily,
My life would be quite different.
I do not understand why I behaved so at that time.

## 씨앗 속에는

씨앗 속에는 떡잎이 있습니다
떡잎 속에는 한 생애가 다리 뻗을 햇살이 있습니다
햇살 속에는 무심의 강물
강물 속에는 이야기가 있습니다
이야기 속에는 슬프고 고운 색깔이 있습니다
색깔 속에는 더디고 질긴 꿈이 있습니다
꿈속에는 눈물이, 눈물 속에는 소금이 있습니다
소금 속에는, 소금 속에는
저린 삶이 있습니다

내 잡고 서 있는 아흔아홉 현금
어느 것을 울려도 나는 아픕니다

버린 돌멩이 하나
흐르는 세월 속에 놓친 바람 한 조각도
풍랑이 되어 반란이 되어 날 풀어헤칩니다
씨앗이 움켜쥔 정절은
내 기후에 떨어져 뿌리를 내립니다
날개가 됩니다, 기폭이 됩니다, 믿음이 됩니다
독한 삶이 되어 다시
씨앗을 낳습니다

# In A Seed

In a seed there lies a tiny leaf.
In a tiny leaf lies sunlight for its life to be thriven.
In a sunlight, a river of purity.
In a river, a story.
In a story, a color woven into sorrow and beauty.
In a color, a dream steady and endless.
In a dream a tear, and in a tear a salt.
In a salt, in a salt,
There is a life of agony.

Ninety nine strings am I holding,
I could not play a string without a sore heart.

Even a stone cast away there,
A piece of wind lost in the flowing times,
They become a high seas, rebellions to disperse me.
The spirit the seed conceives is sowed
In my soil and its root strikes deep.
It becomes a wing, a banner and a faith.
It becomes a harsh life
And bears the seeds again.

## 저녁 메밀밭

고추잠자리 낮게 뜨고
추억 같은 노을 번져
나는 평생에 처음
화려하게 외롭다

메밀밭 고랑
메밀밭 고랑
눈물 나게 외롭다
왜 우냐 다그치면
말문이 콱 막혀도

문득 스친 손가락이
따스하여서
저녁 메밀밭
저녁 메밀밭
눈물 나게 외롭다

# The Buckwheat Field In The Twilight

When the red dragonflies is flying low,
And an evening glow spreads like a recollection,
I feel lone in full splendour
For the first time in my life.

The buckwheat furrow,
The buckwheat furrow,
I feel lone tearfully.
Though I got struck dumb,
When urged for the reason of the tears.

Suddenly warm hands
Go past by,
The buckwheat field in the twilight,
The buckwheat field in the twilight,
I feel lone tearfully.

# 해바라기

해바라기는 꽃이 아닙니다
꽃이 되려다 못 된 넋들이
입김에도 스러질 연한 것들이
철천지한을 다지고 다져
저렇게 정신 차리고 서 있는 것입니다

발돋움 홰를 쳐도 땅은 낮아라
소리소리 하늘에 다리를 놓아
깃발처럼 머리 풀고 서 있는 것입니다

해는 긴긴날 금실을 꼬아
심장 위에 한 땀 한 땀 바늘을 꽂고
꽃잎보다 슬픈 피 먼저 쏟으며
저렇게 꽃인 듯이 흉내 내는 것입니다

세상의 꽃들은 모두 죽어서
해바라기 되는 것이 소원입니다

# The Sunflower

The sunflower is not a flower,
But a spirit failed to be a flower,
So tender to be vanished even by a breath,
After hardening its deep sorrow and regret,
It is sustaining there, so strained every nerve.

Even tiptoeing or crowing is useless on the low ground.
Putting a ladder to the sky, yelling and shouting,
They are standing with dishevelled hair like a flag.

Sun is spinning golden thread for the long long days,
Needling through their hearts, stitch by stitch,
And shedding blood, more grieved than the petals,
It's posing as it is flower, either.

All the flowers on the earth have the wishes to be
A sunflower in their next world.

## 꽃차를 마시며

꽃차를 마신다
목숨의 한가운데 정수리를 꺾어서
연꽃 송이 우리어 향내에 갇힌다
찻집의 커다란 창 유리에는
이른 봄 는개가 낮게 깊게 흐느끼고
새로 생긴 가슴앓이 숨을 한참 고른 후
사기잔 적막 속에 차를 따른다

이제 나 이렇게 막바지에 왔는가
얼린 꽃 녹여서 향이나 우려
아무렇지 않게
꽃차를 마시다니,
눈 감으면 원도 없지, 무얼 또 바라랴만
나는 또 죄 하나를 쌓고 있는가

## Teaing The Flower Tea

I'm having a flower tea.
Plucking lotus at the supreme freshness of its life,
I'm lost in the fragrance of the flower steeped.
On the wide glass wall of the teahouse
Early spring mist is sobbing, deep and low.
After long stroking down my new heartburn,
I'm pouring the tea into the calm of a porcelain cup.

How I've come to the near of the extrem limit!
For I'm brewing the frozen lotus, after melting it,
As if nothing is happened,
And enjoying the flower tea.
Though I've nothing to wish when I shut my eyes,
Am I heaping up a new sin to my former ones?

## 여름 산을 바라보고 있으면

여름 산을 바라보고 있으면
죽는다는 것이
하나도 무섭지 않다
죽는다는 것은
호사스런 저 산자락을 베고 눕는 일
갈증에 울먹이던 저잣거리
두 발목 잡아끄는 수렁을 지나
연기처럼 굴뚝을 벗어나는 일
연기처럼 긴 머리채 헤뜨리고서
벙어리 저 들녘을 내려다보는 일
피리새 패랭이꽃 훨훨한 구름
비로소 나도
평화로운 한 칸 마루 정자를 짓는 일
멀리 여름 산
고매한 눈길을 쫓아가노라면
죽는다는 것이
하나도 두렵지 않다

# When I Look At The Summer Mountain

When I look at the summer mountain,
I am not the least afraid
To meet my end.
Dying is simply to rest my head
On that luxury mountain edge.
Passing through the marketplace crying for thirst,
And a swamp pulling me by legs,
It's a vanishing away from the chimney like a smoke.
Dying is, just looking down at the mute field,
With the long hair dishevelled like a smoke.
The finches, the wild pinks, and the clouds floating free.
At last I am also
Building a small floor bower of peace.
When I gaze with the lofty eyesight
On the summer mountain far away,
I am not the least afraid
To meet my end.

## 풀꽃

어디서 보았을까
낯익은 얼굴

해산한 여인 같은
가을 들판에
한나절 해를 묶어
들러 가게 하는
그대

천지 분간도 못 하던 그때
칼로 벤 듯, 하직하듯
돌아섰을 때
내 발등 적시는 눈물
닦아 내던 사람

산천을 떠돌았지
소금밭에 누웠었지
철들면 안다는 말
믿지 않았지

## The Weed Flower

Where did I see you before?
You are a familiar face.

At an autumn field,
Like a woman after childbirth,
Holding sun of half a day,
And letting it drop in,
You are.

At the time I could not distinguish the world,
When I turned backward,
As if cutting with sword and parting him,
You wiped off my feet
Which were stained with tears.

I was wandering about the mount and river.
I was lying down on the salt field.
A tale that it'll be understood after discretion,
I would not believe such a folklore.

저물어 돌아오는 지친 발아래
옛날이나 지금이나
기다리는 이

난장판 보리 꺼풀
나 같은 것을
금빛 노을 관을 쓰고
바라보는 이

먼 산자락 끌어 덮어
다독이면서
잊었는가
잊었겠지
꿈을 꾸라 하는 이

Under my weary feet returning home at dusk,
From bygone till now,
You are always waiting for me.

At a person like me,
A mere barley bran at marketplace,
You, weed flower, are gazing up,
Wearing a crown of golden evening glow.

You are pulling, quilting yonder mount edge,
And patting me on the shoulder, saying,
"Have you forgotten it?
Surely you've done.
Now dream a new dream."

# 깊은 잠

나를 좀 도와주세요
잘 때도 두 손은
이 세상 언덕 위에 얹어 놓고 잡니다
해면 같은 잠이 동굴보다 깊어
사정없는 몽유 속으로 날 끌어들입니다

아침 해안 지푸라기 하나를
기적처럼 움켜쥐려고
그 어둠 속 완전한 침몰을 막으려고
두 손만이라도 성하게 살리려고 그럽니다
내 소원을 들어주세요

밤이 독약처럼 밀려옵니다
숨 쉬면 먹물이 목줄기를 깎아내립니다
죽고 사는 일
다 뜻이 있음을 믿습니다만
매일 아침 살아남는 일이
정말 같지가 않습니다

돌아다보아 주십시오
이 절절한 벼랑에서
눈을 뜨는 나를

## Sound Slumber

May you help me.
Even when I'm sleeping,
My hands are always laid on this earthly hills.
My sweet slumber is deeper than the cave
And draws me severely into the deep dream.

To grasp a straw at morn shore
So miraculously,
To save my complete sinking down into that darkness,
I'm trying to keep my hands alive as always they are.
May you grant my wishes.

A night is surging upon me like a poison.
Black water hurts my throat during breathing.
The matter of dying or living,
I believe, it belongs to the will of the Almighty,
Yet, I wonder how, every morn,
I could be left alive.

May you look back at me
Awakening to a sense
On the edge of this lofty cliff.

제2부

# 세상의 후미진 곳에서

*part* 2

# At The Deeply Secluded Place

## 안부

자네도 알지
'데스가부도'라는 사람
군산 사람이면 누구나 알 것이네
해망동 굴 밖 비릿한 뱃고동 소리에
수박덩이만 한 머리통을 가누고
비 오는 부두에서 군가를 부르던
그 총각

많이 늙었다데
비단 폭 밟듯, 예수처럼
바다를 밟고 싶어 하며
평화롭게 마흔 살도 넘었다데

초등학교 뒷담 밑은
우리들의 왕궁
'야, 데스가부도다, 미친놈! 설친 놈!'
조무래기들은 침을 뱉으며
팔매질하며
그러면 데스가부도는
'저리들 가! 느이들 미쳤냐? 미쳤어?'

## Warm Regards

Surely you know the man called by 'Daethgabudo'*
None doesn't know him, there in Gunsan.
Out the Haemangdong tunnel,
Keeping his head steady, as big as a watermelon,
Along the quayside in the rain,
Singing a military march to the fishy boat horn,
Was the lad.

Guess he became old enough.
As if on a silky texture, likewise Jesus did,
Wishing to tread on the sea,
Now he has gone over forty years in peace.

It was our Kingdom
Under the wall of primary school.
'Look, it's Daethgabudo, crazy! you raver!'
The kiddies were spitting,
Throwing stones to him.
Then, Daethgabudo said usually,
'Get out! Are you mad? you crazy?'

아! 그의 절규가
헛바람처럼 맴돌던 초록 하늘
정녕 아름답던 초록 하늘엔
비행기 몇 대가 날고 있었지
나보다
먼저 죽고 말 것이네
그는

대추나무 잔가지로 수액이 뻗치듯
천천한 내 사랑은 전할 길이 없이……

우리들은 소망대로 어른이 되고
우리들의 어린 것들은 골목에서
흙 묻어 크네

내 비망록 저 은밀한 부분에서
데스가부도가 억울하게 늙어 가네

Oh, his outcries were whirling
Into the blue sky like an empty wind.
Over the sky so beautiful in blue
A few planes were flying away.
Surely I believe,
Before me,
He would die.

My love as steady as the sap reaching-up in jujube twigs,
There's no way to send it to him……

We became grown up as expected
And our children are also growing up,
Covered with mud and earth.

In a secret page of my memorandum
Daethgabudo is growing older, unfairly.

* Deathgabudo : Japanese pronunciation for military steel helmet.

# 유서를 쓰던 밤

내게도 유서를 쓰던 밤이 있었지
앞길 창창하던 젊은 시절
어둠은 궁성같이 거룩하고
고요는 뻘밭처럼 끈끈했었지

나는 생애의 마지막 밤을
포옹하면서
달개비꽃 맑은
나의 별을 우러렀었지

나의 유서는 차라리
아름다운 연서
세상을 목숨 바쳐 사랑했었네
온몸이 무너지는 고백이었지

댓돌 위에 벗어 놓은
이승의 신발 위에
달빛 가득 흐느끼던 나의 첫사랑
유서를 쓰던 밤의 위태롭던 꿈
내 평생 가장 추운 밤이었었지

# The Night When I Wrote A Will

Once I had a night when I wrote a will
At my youth of the bright future ahead.
The darkness was even holy like a royal castle,
The tranquility was as sticky as mud.

Then, I embraced
The last night of my life
And admired my star
As clear as a commelina.

My will was rather
A beautiful love letter,
For I'd loved the world with all my heart.
It was a confession, done by collapsing myself.

Upon my shoes in this world
Which were left on the stepstone,
The moonlight was shadding, sobbing for my first love.
A perilous dream at night when I wrote my will,
It was the chilliest night in my life.

## 찻잔의 모서리에

찻잔의 모서리에 입술연지가 묻었다
커피는 벌써 아득히
나도 모를 후미진 골목으로 스며들고
입술 자국만 각인처럼 남았다
돌아서서 몰래 입술연지를 지운다
허락되지 않은 열정을 간음이라 했지
간음의 흔적처럼 부끄러운 자리
손바닥 가려 하늘을 속이듯
손바닥 가려 내 죄를 감추듯
남들이 다 손가락질하는
쓸어안고 울고 싶은 어두운 운명 같은
찻잔의 모서리 입술연지
살다가 떨어뜨린 이삭 같은 것이
더러는 남아 있을 연지 자국 같은 것이
하늘 아래 유별나게 두드러지는
하늘 아래 유별나게 펄럭거리는
아, 사는 일이 이렇게 투명하구나

# On The Rim Of A Cup

On the rim of a cup there rouged by a lipstick.
The coffee already vanished into
Far away remout alley,
And a rouge stain was left on the cup like a seal.
I turned and cleaned the mark on the cup silently.
It is said the forbidden passion is an adultery.
It was a stain of shame like an adultery mark
As if to deceive heaven, covering it by hands,
As if to hide the sins by hands.
A dark fate that I wish to embrace and wail over,
Scorned by others,
You, a lipstick on the rim of a cup,
Like an ear of grain dropped during my life,
Like a lipstick remained usually on the rim.
Notable distinctively under the sky,
Fluttering distinctively under the sky,
Ah, it is thus clear to lead a life!

# 아름다운 목소리로 후회하고 싶었다

단감나무 서너 그루 삼신처럼 심어 놓고
마른 풀내 향기로운 띳집이 한 채
까치 떼 모여드는 고목나무처럼
나도 점잖게 나이 들고 싶었다
허드레 우물 지나서 미나리 방죽 지나서
나지막한 굴뚝, 파묻히는 흙담 밑에
어디서 누가 나를 부르나
물살 위에 흔들리는 추억 같은 무늬
외풍 없는 남향의 외할머네 마당에
옛날처럼 내가 돌아와 서면
내 탯줄 살라서 묻어 둔 산이
턱밑에 당긴 듯 가까웠었다
푸르른 연기가 몸을 뒤틀어
아슴한 바람벽을 핥고 가는 저녁
나는 너무 오래 헤매었구나
두 무릎 사이에 얼굴을 묻고
아름다운 목소리로 후회하고 싶었다

# I Wished To Repent Myself With A Sweet Voice

A few sweet persimmon trees planted like three spirits[*]
And a thatched cottage scenting of dry grass,
I wished to be aged gently
As an old tree where a flock of magpies are flying in.
By the unuseful well and the bed of water parsley,
At the low chimney, the clay wall sunken into the earth
There supposed someone called me.
The figures like a recollection waving on the comber.
When I returned and stood, as I did in my past time,
At my grandma's garden facing south, without draft,
The hill was near as beneath my chin,
Where my navel string was burned and buried.
In the even when the blueish smock was twisting itself
And crawling up on the foggy wall,
I found myself wandering about so long.
I wished to repent myself with a sweet voice,
burying my face between the laps.

---

[*] The three spirits : Korean legendary three spirits governing child birth.

# 봄밤

꽃이 핀다

우리도 꽃 피자
우리도 꽃 피자
신열로 부대끼는 마을 사람들
뜬눈으로 울력하는
긴긴
봄

나이 찬 뒤뜰의 살구나무는
분내 나는 무릎으로
분내 나는 무릎으로
얼었던 창마다 불을 켜 댄다
조그맣게 우는 소리
꽃이 핀다

꽃이 핀다
죽는 일처럼 사는 일처럼
말이 쉽지
꽃 피는 게 어디 예삿일인가

# Spring Night

The blossoms are blooming.

Let us also blow now.
Let us also blow now.
The villagers are harassed with ardor,
Without a blink of nap with eagerness
For a long, long
Spring time.

The aged apricot tree in the back yard is
With its root of scent,
With its trunk of scent,
Illuminating all the frozen windows on every spray.
With a silent sobbing
They are blooming.

They are blooming
Like a matter of dying, like a matter of living.
You say it easily,
But is it an occurring everyday to bloom?

봄밤
꽃이 핀다

At spring night

The blossoms are blooming.

# 꽃

꽃이라고 소리내기까지
나는 숱한 말을 더듬거렸습니다
꽃이라고 소리 낸 다음
나는 다른 말을 죄 잊어버렸습니다
꽃이란 말이 독바늘처럼
귀에 와 꽂히는 뜻을 알겠지요

고운 피로, 아니면 어지러운 연기로
꽃이여, 벙어리여
있는 것 다 털어 날려 보내고
울부짖을 목청도 없이
두 손을 헤저으며 돌아온 것이여

내 화첩에는 꽃만 남았습니다

날개 달린 새들이야 애진즉 날아가고
네발 달린 짐승은 걸어서 갔습니다
묶이어 만만한 꽃
육합에 가득 꽃만 남았습니다

# The Flower

Till I voiced "Flower",
I stammered over the numerous words.
After I breathed "Flower"
I have forgotten all of the other words.
You understand why the word of Flower is
Surely stuck in my ears like a poisoned needle.

A sweet blood, a foggy smock,
You, Flower, a mute!
You have blown away all of your merit and virtue,
And even without a voice to yell,
You returned, rummaging your hands so long!

In my picture book there left the Flower only.

The winged birds already flew away,
The four footed animals fled away.
You, Flower, tied up, so easy,
There are full of the flowers in the world.

목젖 밑에 두고두고 삭아 내리는
흐느낌 같은, 바람 소리 같은
기도만 몇 마디 남았습니다

Like a sobbing fermented down slowly under the throat,
Like a weak murmuring of the wind,
There remained only a few words of prayer.

# 저녁 강가에서

저녁 강가에 서면
누구에겐가 혼신으로 예배하고 싶다
고별의 하루 해 가슴에 파묻고
목숨 바쳐 누군가를 사랑하고 싶다

정박한 배들이 찢어진 돛폭을 꿰매어
전설의 바다 산호섬을 꿈꿀 때
쓸쓸하다, 저녁 강가에 서면
노을은
하혈의 현기증으로 물결을 덮고
돌아다보는 기억들은 꽃밭보다 곱다

저녁 강가에 서면
하늘 아래 한 사람의 이름을 외워
'영원히'라고 맹세하고 싶다

강물은 만삭의 여인처럼
가쁜 숨을 쉬고
나는 내일 아침
새순처럼 부활하고 싶다

# By The Riverside At Eventide

Whenever I stand by the riverside at eventide
I wish to worship someone with whole my soul.
Burying the departing sun deep in my heart
I wish to love somebody with whole my life.

While they are patching the sails on the anchored boats
And dreaming a coral island on the legendary sea,
I'm lone, whenever I stand by the riverside at eventide.
The glow of the sunset is
Spreading over the waves with bloody dizziness
And the past memories are more gorgeous than a blossom.

Whenever I stand by the riverside at eventide
I wish to learn by heart one's name under the skies
And make a solemn vow, 'Forever'.

The river gasps
Like a parturient woman
And at morrow morn
I wish to revive like a new bud.

성전처럼 가라앉은
저녁 강가에 서면

Whenever I stand by the riverside at eventide

Which is calmed down in tranquility like sacred shrine.

# 연연

내 비록 하루 세끼
밥은 먹고 살아도,
내 소망은 새가 되는 일.
내가 믿는 것은
당신과의 약속.

어느 날 홀연히 날 불러도
그 소리 듣지 못한 채
귀먹어 있으면 어쩌나,
어쩌나,

그 외 딴 걱정은 없습니다
걱정 없습니다

# Lingering Affections

Even though I'm making my life barely
By three meals a day,
I wish I'm a bird.
What I'm believing is
A promise tied with you.

Some day when you call me
And suddenly I can not hear your voices
As I become a deaf,
What, what shall I do?

Except that, I've nothing to worry about,
Never, never a problem!

# 세상의 후미진 곳에서

이 세상 후미진 곳에서
나를 아직 용서하지 못하는
사람이 있나 보다
용서할 수 없음에 뜬눈의 밤이 길고
나처럼 일어나서
불을 켜는 사람이 있나 보다

질펀히 젖어 있는 창문께로 가서
목 늘여 달빛을 들이마시면
나를 적셔 흐르는 깨끗한 물살
반가운 소식처럼 퍼지는
예감

나를 용서하지 않는 사람이 있나 보다
용서받지 못할 일을 내가 저질렀나 보다
그의 눈물 때문에 온종일 날이 궂고
바람은 서러워 온몸으로 우나 보다
사시 철 그래서 내 마음이 춥고
바람결 소식에도 귀가 시린가 보다

# At The Deeply Secluded Place

At the deeply secluded place
It seems there is a person
Who would not forgive me yet.
He sits up all night for his unforgiving mind,
Who gets up
And light up as I do.

When I come near to the window flooded with moonlight
And drink it by my neck stretched out
The pure water wets and flows me down,
Spreading, like a good news,
Its premonition.

It seems somebody would not forgive me.
Maybe I made a mistake unable to be forgiven.
Maybe it is rainy all day long caused by his tears,
And wind is sobbing so sorrowfully, shaking its frame.
Maybe I feel cold in my heart through the year
And my ears feel cold even by a hearsay in the wind.

## 나는 지금 다시

나는 지금 다시 잠들려고 합니다
일몰의 그늘에서 깃발을 내리듯
순순한 육신을 꽃가지처럼 드리우고
활개 쳐선 갈 수 없는 요요한 꿈속으로
새털같이 즐겁게 떠나려고 합니다

사실 지금 다시 잠들지 않아도
나는 사철 잠들어 있었습니다
눈뜬 자의 지혜에 불을 켜지 못하고
산 자의 고요가
독약보다 슬프게 퍼지는 것을
장승처럼 그냥 서서 보았습니다

이제 새삼 잠든다는 것은
우스운 일입니다
이제 거듭 잠든다는 것은
무서운 일입니다
이 절정의 죄짓는 나를
흔들어 주십시오

제발 이 막판의 어리석은 나를
매질하여 주십시오

# I'm Going To Fall Asleep Again

I'm going to fall asleep again.
As if a flag is taken down at the sunset shadow,
I'm spreading my weak body like a sprig of flowers.
Into the faraway dream beyond the wings' reach,
I'll leave as joyfully as a feather.

In fact, though I do not fall asleep now again,
I've been sleeping all the year round.
Unable to light up the wisdom of the awakened,
But the silence of the alive is spreading out
More sorrowfully than the poison,
I could not but wait to see it like a totem pole.

To fall asleep anew after so long time,
It is ridiculous.
To fall asleep over again,
It is dreadful.
From committing the worst sin
Please shake and awake me up.

For my foolishness at this last chance
Please whip me.

# 내 가슴 등잔에 불을 댕겨서

달력 한 장이
이 겨울 단 하나 소망처럼 남았습니다.
우리는 기다립니다
축복처럼 하얀 눈길을 타고
이 세상 종악을 모두 울리면서
당신이 오시기를

그날 이별을 바라보던 식탁에서
같은 떡 그릇에 손을 담글 때
어리석은 우리들 배반의 날을
슬프게 슬프게 예언하시던 분
그날 검게 찢어지는 휘장 아래서
다투어 옷가지를 찢어 가질 때
죽어도 백 번 불쌍한 목숨들을
슬프게 슬프게 축복하시던 분

끝끝내 홀로 남은 잎새 같은 달력이
쓸쓸한 결심처럼 흔들리며 있습니다

내 가슴 등잔에 불을 댕겨서
당신이 오실 길을 밝히고 싶습니다

# By Kindling A Lantern In My Heart

The one page of the calendar is left
As if it's the only one hope in this winter.
We are waiting,
Passing through the way of white snow of grace,
Pealing out all the bells in the world,
You will come to us.

That day, at the supper table, foreseeing their parting,
When they dipped the bread into the same bowl,
You prophesied the time of our foolish betrayals
With sorrow, so deep sorrow.
That day, under the black curtain torn into two pieces,
When they quarrelled with your clothes to tear and divide,
You blessed the souls poorest after centuple death,
With sorrow, so deep sorrow.

The last page of the calendar is, like a last leaf,
Fluttering by itself like a lone decision.

By kindling a lantern in my heart
I wish to brighten up along the ways of your coming.

# 날궂이

날이 궂었다 하면 맨발로 행군하던 남자
온 동네 손가락질하던 '미친놈'
청년에 죽었으므로 그는 여태 청년이다

꽃이 지는 봄 저녁
처녀는 지는 꽃잎을 깔고 앉아 헤실거렸다
해는 어슬어슬하고 깨알로 박아 쓴 편지는
통분의 고소장
어려운 손님처럼 몸을 꼬았다
입에 담지 못할 끔찍한 일을 당했다는 소문
미치지 않고는 죽는 길밖에 없었다는 소문
가늘게 떨리던 그녀의 희고 고운 손가락

나는 미친 사람들과 친하다
어디를 가나 미친 사람들과 한통속이 된다
성한 사람들이 미친 사람보다 더 미친 짓을 하는 세상에
정녕 이러다가 내가 미치지, 그럴 바에야 진작 그럴 걸
하늘이 끄느름 날궂이를 하고
나는 지금 맨발로 뛰쳐나가고 싶다

# The Foul Day

A man, marching barefoot whenever it was a foul day.
"Crazy guy", who was scorned by the whole village.
He is young yet because he died young.

In the spring even when petals were falling,
The maiden was sitting on petals with silly smiles.
At dusk, a letter written by minute handwriting,
Rather a wrathful letter of complaint would it be.
She fidgeted herself as an uncomfortable guest does.
A rumor that she was assaulted in an unutterable cruelties,
No other way than dying was there, except going mad.
Her white and pretty hands were trembling feebly.

I'm on good terms of intimacy with the crazy ones.
I become a companion with the insane wherever I go.
Many healthy people behave madly more than the mad,
Surely I may be mad thus, then I should be so earlier.
The dusky sky is getting foul.
I wish to dash out barefoot.

# 어디 갔을까

고무신 한 켤레 가지런한 강둑
임자는 벗어 놓고 멀리 갔는가
풀들은 간밤 비에 늘펴하게 자빠지고
빗물이나 공연히 출렁대면서
내일은 관을 쓰고 옥당에 닿더라도
나 더는 걸을 수 없다
온몸을 비틀어 소리소리 지르는가
치마폭 뒤집어 강물 위에 꽂고
하얀 단속곳 너울처럼 둘러
장화와 홍련 물귀신이 되었을까
용궁으로 가는 인당수에 빠져서
심학규 외동딸 청이처럼 돌아올까
성한 신발 두 짝 나란한 강둑
빗물로 써 내린 서슬 푸른 유서
임자는 왜 여태 돌아오지 않는가

# I Wonder Where You'd Gone

On the bank placed a pair of rubber shoes.
The owner may have gone far away barefoot.
The grass drooped with the rain last night.
The rainwater was waving needlessly.
"If I may arrive at the palace morrow on crown,
I could not walk anymore",
Are you crying out by twisting the whole body?
By drowning yourself in the river with the skirt up,
And whirling the white underwear like a veil,
You became a water spirit of ChangWha, HongRyon?
After sunken into the Indang, to the sea palace,
Would you return back as Chung, daughter of the blind?
On the bank placed a pair of rubber shoes.
The mighty last will written down by the rain.
Why wouldn't you return back yet?

제3부

# 아침에는 이슬이

*part 3*

## The Dewdrops In The Morn

# 문패

우리 집 문패는 작고 초라하다
남 보기에 하찮을 우리 행복의 크기
남편의 고집이 내 순종을 불러
거기 휘파람 불며 걸려 있다
'이 담에 대리석 기둥에
당신 이름이랑 함께 새겨서'
그가 몇 해 전이던가 말했었다

문밖은 꽤 차고
이따금 바람 지나는 소리도 들렸었다
나는 웃었다
벌써 중년에 접어든 그의 얼굴은 안 보고 가만히 웃었다
벌써 중년에 접어든
내 웃는 얼굴을 보고
그가 어떤 얼굴을 하였나 나는 보지 못했다

## The Name Plate

Our name plate is tiny and even shabby,
As the size of our happiness, so trifling to others.
By his insisting that extracted my obedience
It is hung there whistling on the doorway.
"Someday let it be with your name
On a marble wall",
He said some years ago.

Bitterly cold was it there outside
And sometimes heard the wind passing.
I smiled,
Without looking at his middle aged face.
At my smiling face,
Already set in a middle age,
How was his feeling, I did not know.

# 편지

오밤중에 이 편지를 씁니다
밀밀한 수목의 울음소리같이
깊고 크낙한 그믐밤에

길길이 쌓인 나의 염원은
금세 젖어 버린 핏빛 손수건

이 소식을 전합니다

이 밤 어느 집 뜰에서는
한 알 앙증스런 봉숭아 씨가 영그는데
다 아신다면서 아무것도 모르시는 당신

이 같은 밤엔 나도 남루한 옷을 갈아입고
양지바른 땅 향 어린 수목으로
피어나고 싶습니다

이 사연을 전합니다

# A Letter

In a midnight I'm writing this letter,
Like a crying of the thick forest,
At the last night of a month, deep and huge.

The dearest wishes heaped up in my heart is
A handkerchief wet so soon in crimson blood.

I'm sending this letter.

Tonight, in the yard of a neighbor
An exquisite seed of garden balsam is ripening,
You know nothing, while you've pretended to know all.

In such a night I would dress up myself out of rags
And bloom into a fragrant tree
In a sunny place.

I'm sending this letter with my crimson heart.

# 어머니의 밥

"애야 밥 먹어라"
어머니의 성경책
잠언의 몇 절쯤에
혹은 요한계시록 어디쯤에
금빛 실로 수를 놓은
이 말씀이 있을 거다

"애야, 밥 먹어라
더운 국에 밥 몇 술 뜨고 가거라"
아이 낳고 첫국밥을 먹은 듯
첫국밥 잡수시고 내게 물리신
당신이 젖을 빨고 나온 듯
기운차게 대문을 나서는 새벽.

맑은 백자 물대접만한
유순한 달이 어머니의 심부름을 따라 나와서
"체할라 물 마셔라, 끼니 거르지 말거라"
눈앞 보얗게 타일러 쌓고
언제부터서인가
시원의 검은 흙바닥에서부턴가
마른 가슴 헐어 내는

## The Meals Of Mom

"Dear, let's have a meal."
You could find these heartful breath from mom's bible,
Embroidered in golden thread,
Somewhere in the verses of
The Proverbs, or,
The Revelations.

"Dear, please have a meal the rices.
You can leave after a few spoons with warm soup."
As if it was the first seaweed soup when my baby birth,
As if I'd sucked your breast you fed
After you'd had the first seaweed soup,
At dawn I was passing the gate with full of strength.

Amiable moon, a white big bowl,
Follows me by her errand, saying repeatedly,
"Drink water for your digestion, don't miss a meal."
By your warm advice my eyes become foggy with tears,
From some time or other,
From the depth of black earth in the Beginning, maybe,
Your cares are

당신의 근심
평생토록 밥을 먹이는
당신의 사랑

Pulling down your thin breast.

Your love is

Feeding me to the end of your life.

# 동행

강물이여
눈먼 나를 데리고 어디로 좀 가자
서늘한 젊음, 고즈넉한 운율 위에
날 띄우고
머리칼에 와서 우짖는 햇살
가늘고 긴 눈물과
근심의 향기
데리고 함께 가자

달아나는 시간의 살침에 맞아
쇠잔한 육신의 몇십 분의 얼마
감추어 꾸려 둔 잔잔한 기운으로
피어나리

강물이여 흐르자
천지에 흩어진 내 목숨 걷어
그중 화창한 물굽이 한 곡조로
살아남으리

진실로 가자
들녘이고 바다고
눈먼 나를 데리고 어디로 좀 가자

# Companion

You, River,
Take me, a blind, to anywhere.
Float me, a fresh youth,
On a calm and cozy note.
With the sunbeams shouting on my hair,
Long and thin tears,
And a fragrance of anxiety,
Take me along with all of these.

With the strength, a pinch of several tithes,
Concealed and saved from the weakened muscles
Shot by the arrow of time running away,
I will come in full blossoms.

You, River, let us flow.
Gathering my soul scattered in the world,
And then, as a note of the dazzling waves
I will leave alive.

Now, really, let's flow
To the sea, even to the plain.
Take me, a blind, to anywhere.

# 내 가슴의 고요

너를 바라보는
내 가슴의 고요에서는
낮은 풍금 소리가 난다

낙엽은 사철
아름다운 사연의
엽서처럼 지고

그 발자욱마다 기도로 스미리
풍화하는 노래로 잠기리
함께 가는 강물의 유유함이여
함께 가는 햇살의 눈부심이여

너를 생각하는
내 가슴의 고요는
살구 꽃잎 흩날리는
4월 훈풍 같다

땅 위에 이런 은혜
다시 없으리

# The Serenity Of My Heart

In the serenity of my heart
Looking up at you,
There sounds an organ in undertone.

The falling leaves are always
Shedding as if they are
The postcards full of beautiful stories.

On every step it would be seeped with prayer,
Filled with the weathering songs.
The leisure of river, flowing together,
The glare of sunbeams, joining together.

The serenity of my heart
Considering of you,
It resembles the sweet breeze in April,
Which is scattering apricot petals.

There would be no blessing on earth
More than such a blessing.

눈물 가득 너를 보는
내 가슴의 고요

The serenity of my heart
Looking up at you with full of tears.

# 빨래를 널고서

빨래를 널었다
사지를 늘어뜨린
나의 육신을
창천에 표백하듯
내다 걸었다

항복하는 사람처럼
두 팔을 들고
사모하기에는 아직 눈부신
오늘은 해를 향해
가슴을 풀었다

지금 나는 별로 큰
소원도 없고
그렇다고 흐느끼게
설운 일도 없지만
그리움을 알리는
하얀 깃발 하나는
마지막 별처럼 떠 있게
하고 싶다

# I Hung Out The Washes

I hung out the washes.
My body
That was dropping the limbs down
As if bleaching themselves under the sun,
I hung out on a clothesline.

Seemingly to surrender
They raised the hands up
And opened the breast
Towards the sun,
Who is too bright to long for.

At present
I have not any wish utterable,
Not a sorrow
To sob, either.
But I have the dearest wish
To raise up it floated,
A white flag to tell some longings,
As if it is the last star.

빨래를 널었다
제풀에 마르는 들풀처럼
누워서
유순한 복종으로
흔들리고 싶다

I hung out the washes.

I wish to lie down

And to be swayed

Like the grass drying by themselves,

With a gentle obedience.

## 아침에는 이슬이

아침에는 이슬이
저녁에는 안개가
나도 이만하면
넉넉합니다

햇살은 너그럽고
새들은 짖어 쌓고
나도 이만하면
화려합니다

가다가다 눈먼 바람
평지를 막고
빈 들판 질러가던
그대 흙신발
어느새 돌아와
서성댑니다

내 가슴 복판에서
서성댑니다

# The Dewdrops In The Morn

The dewdrops in the morn,
The mists in the even,
These are so much
For me.

The sunlight generous,
The birds twittering,
These are so splendid
For me.

The blind winds are, now and then,
Blocking the ground.
Passing through the empty field,
You, wearing muddy dauby shoes,
Returned so soon,
And hanging around.

Deep in the middle of my heart
You are hanging around.

## 저녁 산

저녁 산이 앓는 것을
모를 뻔하였네

긴긴 낮 하늘
떠받쳐 올리던 장대
저녁이면 고단해서
휘청거리는 것을

피 묻어나겠네
자지러지는 노을
저녁 산 바라 타오르고
타는 노을 턱 밑에서
저녁 산 앓는 것을
모를 뻔하였네

걸어서 하루, 짱짱한 백 리
제 그림자 걷어들이는
저녁 산 발걸음을
하루치 어스름
몇 마을의 위안
나갔던 새들 불러들이는

# The Even Mount

The mount is moaning in the even
I nearly didn't know it.

The pole, lifting up the sky
During that long long daylight,
Is exhausted toward even
And tottering.

Seemingly soaked with its blood,
The frightened glow of sunset
Is burning against the even mount.
At the near by the burning glow
The even mount is moaning,
I nearly didn't know it.

A day's walk, a quarter of a hundred mile or more,
The heavy tread of the even mount which is
Rolling up its own shadow.
A day's dusk,
A comfort from a few villages,
Calling in the birds which were fled away,

저녁 산 쉰 목소리를

산이 저녁에 앓는 것을 모를 뻔하였네
산이 저녁으로 늙는 것을 모를 뻔하였네

The hoarsened voices from the mount in the even.

I nearly didn't know a moan of a mount in the even.
I nearly didn't know an aging of a mount in the even.

## 집으로 간다

식구들이 모두 돌아왔을까
이젠 오늘을 마감해도 좋은가
아침마다 가출했다가
저녁마다 참회하듯 다시 돌아와
떨리는 손가락으로 초인종을 누른다
집은 내 열등한 발목
발목을 잡아끄는 동아줄
사막과 얼음산과 가시덩굴을 넘어
이리와 승냥이와 여우굴을 지나
나 돌아왔노라
시리고 아픈 이름 가족이여
이렇게 돌아올 집이 있노라
저녁 식탁엔 눈물이 안개처럼 자욱하고
그러나 우린 다시 내일의 가출을 음모하면서
각각 제 방으로 타인들처럼 흩어졌다

# I'm Going Home

Did the members of family come home?
Is it good enough for me to close the day?
Every morning I run away from home,
Every evening return home like a repenter,
And ringing the bell with a trembling finger.
Home is a rope tied on my weakened legs.
It is dragging me toward it.
Passing over the desert, iceberg and thornbush,
Passing by the dens of wolf, coyote and fox,
I've come back home.
The family, the name of chilling and aching,
I've a home to return.
At dinner table there were tears dense like a mist.
But after plotting to run away again tomorrow,
We scattered to their rooms as strangers did.

## 자족하기

이만하면 되었습니다
아름다운 날씨에 하늘빛을 즐기고
바삐 뛰어다닐 두 다리도 성합니다
저녁이면 돌아갈 집이 있고
돌아가서 먹을 저녁밥도 있습니다
기다릴 가족이 있고
머리 숙여 간구할 소원도 있으며
소원을 들어달란 속 깊은 눈물
없는 것 없습니다, 다 있습니다
더러는 원망과 미움이다가
뜨거운 용서와 아픈 후회와
겨운 정에 흐느끼는 강물 같은 가슴
때때로 궁핍으로 날 단련하시고
거기서 강건한 힘도 주시니
아무 불평 없습니다, 다 압니다
쓰러지는 움막에선 흙냄새를 사랑하고
샹들리에 천장 아래 현금을 켜게 하는
아, 크신 은총이여
나는 이만하면 되었습니다

# To Be Self-sufficient

It is sufficient for me,
Enjoying the blue sky on a pleasant weather,
With two healthy legs I can run eagerly.
I've home to return at dusk,
At home supper is waiting for me,
And family also waiting for me to return.
I've wishes to pray with a respectful bow,
With deep heartful tears.
I'm lacking in nothing, everything in abundance.
Sometimes the resentment, hatred arrest me,
But soon comes heartful forgiveness, painful regret,
You are providing me the heart of river, full of affection.
At times you temper me with poverty,
Where you make me stronger than before,
I've no complaint, cause I know you well.
Loving a sniff of earth from an antiquated mud hut,
Playing strings under the chandelier,
Oh, what a wonderful grace of yours on me!
These are more than enough for me!

## 진실하게 말하려면 눈물이 나온다

어제는 타관에서 아들이 다녀갔고
오늘 아침 눈을 뜨자 전화로 물었다
잘 도착했느냐, 너를 만난 어제가 꿈속 같구나
그까짓 말을 하는데도 눈물이 나왔다
세상만사 그중에도 사랑하는 일이여
그래도 전화니까
내가 우나 어쩌나 그 앤 몰랐을 거다

출근하여, 벌써 한 달째나
앓아누웠노라는 친구 소식을 들었다
그만하기 얼마나 다행이냐고
이러다가 죽어도 모를 거라고
그까짓 말을 하는데도 눈물이 또 나왔다
축복이여, 이 세상 도처에 다행스런 일들이여

그러나 전화니까
내가 우나 어쩌나 그는 몰랐을 거다
나는 요새 바보처럼 잘 운다
진실하게 말하려면 눈물이 나온다

# I Am Tearing Whenever I'd Say Honestly

Yesterday my son came by to see me from abroad.
This morning on my waking up I phoned, asking
His safe arrival, saying yesterday it was a dream.
I was tearing even by such a trifling talk.
Among the ways of the world, what a love is!
But it was only a phone call.
He could not know whether I sobbed or not.

After back to the office I heard about my friend,
Who was very sick for a month.
It's fortunate that it was not any more;
Maybe we could not know somebody is dead;
I was tearing even by such a trifling soothing.
The blessings! It's spread all over the would!

For it was only a phone call,
She would not know whether I sobbed or not.
These days I am tearing so easily, so foolishly.
I am tearing whenever I would say honestly.

# 오래된 얼굴

해어름 서쪽 하늘을 바라보고 있노라면
서둘러 귀가하는 나귀 방울 소리 들린다
별들은 제 몸을 부수어서 쪽빛 강에 붓고
추연히 젖어 있는 저녁 산자락
이제 후회하는가

노을 비낀 서쪽 산을 바라보고 있노라면
지금 떠나도 도착할 수 없는 곳
걸어 걸어 찾아가는 지름길이 보인다
길가에는 김을 매 둔 두어 두렁 텃밭과
솥단지 걸었던 유년의 각시풀들

남폿불 낮게 켜 단 창문에서는
그 하루 빗금을 달력에 긋고
식구들은 저녁상에 둘러앉아 있겠지
아프게 바라보는 오래된 얼굴
가까이 가까이
그리워라, 심지를 돋우어 올리겠지

## Faces Of Long Familiar

When I'm gazing at the west sky curtained with sunset,
I hear the jingle-jangle bells of an ass hurrying home.
On the indigo river stars pour themselves broken to pieces,
The dreary mountain edges at twilight,
Are you regretful now?

When I'm gazing at the west mountains shone with sunset,
The place you couldn't reach, even if you start right away,
In my mind emerges its shortcut to reach there on feet.
Along the lane, a vegetable garden of a few raws weeded,
The squill, idol bride,[*] playing house in childhood.

Under the oil lamp lit and hung low at the window,
They are drawing a slant line on the date in calendar.
I see the family members around the supper table,
Whose faces of long familiar are in my sore heart.
Come close, more close,
I miss them, and they'll turn up the wick.

---

[*] An idol bride made of squill, the plant. Its root becomes idol's head and hairs, and its body, green leaves become a skirt for the idol bride.

## 이후로도 우리를

네가 세상에 태어나던 날엔
아침부터 까치가 유난히 우짖더니
경이로운 소식처럼 네가 왔다
그날 밤 나는 하나님에게
길고 긴 보은의 편지를 썼다
'신실한 어미가 되게 하소서'
그 후로 내 기운은 칡넝쿨처럼 뻗고
자랑은 여름 갈대밭보다 무성해
아들아,
이것이 너를 둔 행복이었다

이제는 한 소녀를 아름다이 여겨
숨겨 온 사랑을 고백할까 어쩔까
네 순한 가슴은 미열에 떠 있고
그리운 풍경을 멀리서 손짓하듯
나는 너의 뒷모습을 강물처럼 바라본다

오늘은 네가 세상에 태어난 날
나는 다시 간절한 편지를 쓴다
주여, 우리들을 그윽하게 하소서

# Even Since Then For Us

At the date you were born in this world,
The magpies cried out so loud in the morn
And you came to us like a wondrous news.
At that night I wrote a letter to my God,
Long long letter of gratitude,
'Let me be a sincere mom.'
Since then I've gained strength like the arrowroot vines
And my pride was thicker than the summer reeds field.
Dear son,
These have been my happiness caused by you.

At last you fell in love with a lovely girl,
Were shillyshally if you confess your secret love,
And your dovelike breast wandered with fever,
I gazed at your back sight like the river waves,
As if I waved hands for the sweet scene from afar.

Today it's the date you came to us in this world,
Again I write a letter sincerely,
'Please God, let us be deeply occult.'

이후로도 우리를
이후로도 우리를

Let us be so from now on.

Let us be so from now on.

제4부

# 경청하소서

*part* 4

# May You Listen Close To Me

## 해 넘어가기 전

해 넘어가기 전 산마루에는
혼성 코러스의 마지막 소절처럼
혼자서 걸어가는
당신의 뒷모습

깊은 가슴 안창에 암혈을 파고
풀피리 가냘프게 흐느끼면서
당신 얼굴 바로 보면 눈이 멀 것 같아서
어리석게 돌아앉아 죄를 짓는 지금
두려워라
서산에는 하루해가
실없이 넘어가고
당신이여, 왜 아직도
나를 용서하시는가

# Before Sunset

At top of the hill before sunset,
Like the last bar of a mixed chorus,
Walking alone,
Your appearance from behind.

Digging a cave in my inner heart,
Sobbing feebly like a grass pipe,
Fearing of possibly blinded if I face you straight,
So, committing sins foolishly out of your sight,
I am very afraid of.
Over the west hills
The sun is going insincerely.
Why you forgive me,
Even yet!

## 쪽빛 종말을 생각하며

비 오는 날이면 나는 왜
괜찮다, 괜찮다
자꾸만 전에 없이 너그러워지는 것일까
이러다가 정녕 끝장을 보고야 말려는지
수상쩍은 구름은 낮게 깔리고
아직도 젊은 날의 미열에 떠서
이런 날이면 나는 왜
한 점 아편꽃을 먹은 듯
쪽빛으로 정신이 맑아지는 것일까
길 가다 처마 밑에서
똘물처럼 흐르는 빗물 소리를 듣든지
비를 긋는 창 안에서
비를 맞는 창밖을 바라보면
창세의 씨앗 속인가
세상은 참 조고만 쪽빛
육신은 젖은 솜처럼 가라앉고
살아 오르던 풀기도 눅눅해져서
비 오는 날이면 나는 왜
쪽빛 바다 쪽빛 하늘의
쪽빛으로 헝클어지는
한 종말을 생각하게 되는 것일까

# Thinking About The Indigo Blue End Of The World

Whenever it is rainy,

Why do I be generous, not as before,

Saying, "it's not bad, not so bad".

It seems surely to meet the end of the world.

A suspicious clouds are laid low.

In these rainy days,

Yet, I wonder, in a slight fever of my youth,

As if I am addicted to the poppy petal,

Why my soul becomes clearer in indigo blue.

Under the eaves during on my way home,

Hearing the rain flowing as in a brook, or

Looking in the rainy outside

From the inside of the window sheltered from the rain,

It seems an inside of seed creating the world.

The world is a piece of tiny indigo blue.

My body is sunken down like a wetted cotten,

And the stiffness of the starchy clothes gets damp.

Whenever it is rainy,

Why do I think about the end of the world,

Which is entangled in the indigo blue

Of the indigo blue sea, the indigo blue sky?

## 당신의 피리

나로 하여금
당신의 피리를 삼으소서

맺힌 시름은 풀어서
산 넘어 보내고
노여움은 눌러서
잦아들게 하소서

당신을 사랑하는
나의 자랑만
봄풀처럼 봄풀처럼
일으키소서

나로 하여금
당신의 피리가 되게 하소서

가슴은 비워 꽃그늘도 지고
기다리는 노래로 출렁이게 하소서

## Your Flute

Let me
Be your flute.

You may send my worries over the mount,
After they are untangled.
Let my angers subsided,
After they are controlled.

Only my boast
That I'm loving you,
Let it be raised up,
Like a grass, grass in spring time.

Let me
Be your flute.

Let my waiting songs be waved,
Casting the flower shadows over my empty heart.

당신에게 대답하는
맑은 옥피리
예, 예, 대답하는
순한 옥피리

나로 하여금
당신의 피리를 삼으소서

The clear jade flute
Answering to you.
The docile jade flute,
Answering yes, yes.

Let me
Be your flute.

## 소돔의 여자

나는 하릴없는 소돔의 여자
물 길어 밥하고
아이 품어 기른다

나는 어리석은 소돔의 여자
허울뿐인 사랑에도
가슴 헐어 바치고
마른 땅 흙바람에
가랑잎처럼 운다

젖은 신발 끌고 가는
눈에 익은 골목
목숨아,
목숨아,
물구나무선다

# A Woman Of Sodom

I am, inevitably, a woman of Sodom.
Drawing water, cooking foods,
Embracing and nursing baby.

I am a naive woman of Sodom.
Even to a false love in name only
Devoted myself with bare breast
And sobbed like a withered leaves
By dusty winds on the dried earth.

I am passing through the familiar lane,
Draggling the sweated shoes.
Oh, You, Life!
Oh, You, Life!
I'm standing on my hands.

## 어쩌다 나 같은 것이

어쩌다 나 같은 것이
당신을 만나게 되었는지요
어떤 손이 나를 끌어 당신 앞에 세우고
차마 눈부셔 마주 볼 수도 없는
당신의 부르심에
귀를 열게 했는지요
나는 그것이 참 궁금합니다

수많은 만남과 수많은 이별
수많은 그리움과 수많은 슬픔
그 가운데 문득 기별처럼 오신 당신
어떤 손이 당신의 소망 앞에
시든 잡초 같은 나를 일으켜
사모하라
사랑하라
죽도록 사랑하라
나를 흔들어 깨웠는지요

내가 어쩌다가 당신을 만났는지요
해 아래 풍성한 감람 그늘 아래로
어둔 밤엔 희고 맑은 달빛 아래로

# How I, A Wretched

How I, a wretched,
Happened to be encountered with you.
By whose hand I was led to stand before you,
At your glare I could not dare to look up,
And who made me open my ears
To your calling,
Really I wonder about these.

After a numerous encountering and departing,
After a numerous yearning and grieving,
You burst upon my eyes like a news.
Whose hand, in front of your wishes,
Raised up me, a withered weeds, and encouraged
To long,
To love,
To love to the death,
I wonder who shook me out of these deep slumber.

How could I happen to be encountered with you?
You led me to tread on the dry place,
Under the shadow of plentiful olive trees in the sun,

마른 땅을 골라 딛고 걸어가게 하시는
당신의 힘찬 부르심
고요한 침묵
어쩌다 나 같은 것이
당신을 사랑하게 되었는지요

Under the white and clear moonlight at dark.

Your powerful calling.

Your calm silence.

How could I, a wretched,

Become to love you.

## 돌아다보리

그렇지만 나는 돌아다보리
취한 밤의
검은 물이랑처럼
망해 가는 세상의
향내 나는 손길
내 이름 불러서
나는 못 가리

땅 위의 끝날이
도적처럼 올지라도
믿기지 않아서 돌아다보리
혹시나, 잊지 못해
돌아다보리
성읍은 꽃바다
환호성 같은 불에 잠기고
그렇지만, 어리석어
돌아다보리
역청 꿀물 문질러서
잡아끄는 유혹

## Yet, I Would Look Back

Yet, I would look back.
Like the black tide of
The drunken night,
The outstretched hands of sweet fragrance
Of the perishing world are
Calling me by name,
Hence I would not go away from them.

Even if the last day will come
To this world like a thief,
I would look back, for I'm unable to believe it.
Perhaps, for I'm unable to forget them,
I would look back.
The town itself already turning into a blazing inferno,
It's surrounded by the hurrah of flame,
Yet, foolish enough,
I would look back.
Pasted on me with sticky honey
It is an attractive temptation.

벙어리처럼 두 팔 쳐들고
돌기둥
소금기둥
서서 죽으리

I would raise up the arms, as if a mute does,

Like a stone pillar,

Like a salt pillar,

I would die standing.

## 새 동아줄

다 죽고 입 하나만 남았습니다
맨 나중 부르려고 외워 둔 이름
새파란 꽃불 하나 품고 삽니다

빈혈의 벼랑에 눈 감고 서면
썩은 동아줄은 걷어 가시고
새 동아줄을 내려 주시는 당신
새 동아줄 넝쿨처럼 타고 올라가
별이 되든지 달이 되든지
무엇이든 되게 하시는 당신
세상을 다 무너뜨린 다음에도
솟아날 구멍 하나는 일러 주시는 당신

반생 울며 짜낸 두어 방울 향유 있어
머리채 풀어 풀어 당신 발을 닦으리니
당신의 이름은
깊고 큰 바다
백합꽃 순결한 슬픔입니다

# A New Rope

In me indeed everything was dead except my lips.
The name memorized for calling out at last time,
The one blue flame am I embracing and living on.

When I stand at a dizzy cliff with my eyes shut
You gather up the wornout rope
And bestow a new one.
You let me climb up the rope as tendril does,
And become moon or stars,
Allowing me to be anything as I've wished.
Even after wrecking all the world
You show me a narrow escape to spring up.

A few drops of nard oil extracted tearfully half of life
I'll anoint on your feet, wiping with my hair untied,
For your name is
Deep and huge sea,
And a lily of pure sorrow.

## 좀 더 어리석게

나를 좀 더 어리석게 해 주세요
맨낯을 쳐들고
먼 산 바라 누워도
부끄러움 모르는
허허로운 강물
끄덕이며 흘러가는
순순한 강물이게

남의 미움 눈치 못 채
원수진 일 없고
타산이 어긋나도
속으며 살게

하나님
나를 좀 더 더디더디 해 주세요
칼빛인지 별빛인지
따지지 말고
숨구멍 트인 만큼
감싸 안게 하세요

# A Little More Foolish

Let me be foolish a little more than now.
I'd be so, with a barefaced feature,
Lying down, facing to mountains faraway,
Without any sense of shame.
That broad river, flowing generously,
With its waves nodding gently,
I do wish to be as that river does.

I'm not making an enemy of others
For I am slow to catch on the hatred from them.
When the things are going against to my wishes
Let me live on as deceived.

Please God
Let me be slow, slow footed.
Without arguing about
Whether it's flash of sword or starlight.
As much as I can breathe,
Let me embrace all of them.

속엣말 삭아서
단내처럼 고이게

천둥 번개 가락 맞춰
춤이랑 추게
하나님
나를 좀 더 따스하게 하세요

The inner words of mine, well fermented,
Let them swarm around with fragrance enriched.

Keeping in tune of thunder lightning
Let me dance.
Oh, God,
Let me be a little more warm than now.

## 언제쯤 나는

바람은 오늘도 알맞게 붑니다
작은 꽃들 흔들리어 시절을 열고
들풀도 일어나서 어깨를 부비게
품고 사는 사랑이 차돌처럼 영글어서
향기로운 씨알을 남기고 가게

저녁 해가 강물에 알사탕처럼 부서집니다
죽어 가는 여린 것들의 이름을 불러
내일이 온다고 일러 줍니다
이 밤 지나 새벽길로 당신이 오신다면
어디쯤에서 나는
그대 발길 환하게 불꽃 하나 피울까요
인제쯤이나 나는
그대 이름 외치는 작은 깃발 하나
경축의 날 하늘처럼
펄럭일 수 있을까요

# When Can I ······

It is breezing sweetly today also.
It shakes the tiny flowers to open the seasons,
And grows the weeds to rub their shoulders together.
May the love conceived in the heart be ripened hardly,
And its beautiful seed be born for future.

On the river the setting sun breaks its bead into pieces.
It's calling the names of the soft-hearted ones
And let them realize tomorrow is coming.
If you come down through dawn path after tonight,
Whereabouts can I light a lantern
To brighten up your feet?
When can I prepare a little flag
Shouting out your name,
Like the sky on a celebration day,
And flutter the flag?

## 왕이신 당신

내 말씀의 절반쯤은
거짓 맹세
저렇게 거대한 눈으로 내려다보는
하늘의 푸름과
눈물겨운 내 목숨의 발등상인
검은 땅의 비옥함으로
시퍼렇게, 시퍼렇게
맹세만 했습니다

내 말씀의 절반쯤은
몽매한 욕심
가진 떡 아홉보다
못 가진 떡 하나가 커서
눈먼 새끼 짐승처럼 보챘습니다

당신을 사랑하노라
고백한 그 날 이후
당신은 물론 내 왕이십니다만
허구한 날 문밖에서 노숙을 견디는
아, 외롭고 슬픈 왕이신 당신

# You, My Lord

A half of my words uttered to you till now,
That's been the absurd vows.
By the deep blue of the sky
Looking down with that huge eyes,
By the fertility of the black earth,
The footstool for my tearful thread of life,
I've only made that many vows
Strongly, so strongly.

A half of my words uttered to you till now,
That has been the ignorant avarices.
Like a blind youngling I've asked you for
The one bread seemed bigger than each of nine
Which I'd possessed already.

After the day
When I confessed my love to you,
Naturally you are my Lord, My King.
But enduring to stay out of my door as a homeless,
Oh, you are my lone and sorrowful Lord.

## 우리가 사랑할 수 있다면


우리는 새해에도 사랑할 수 있을 거다
머리칼 봄풀 같은 고개 숙여서
가장 먼 종소리에 생각을 씻고
가장 밝은 별빛 가리켜 약속할 수 있을 거다
우리가 사랑할 수 있다면
우리는 새해에도 아름다울 것이다

동네 빈 밭에는 연 날리는 애들
새가 되어 하늘로 가고 싶은 애들
나도 나도 따라 날며 환호하는 애들
아이야, 너는 어디로 가고 싶으냐
새로 배운 발걸음마다 키는 자꾸 솟아오르고
새로 익히는 말씀마다 다 이루어 주시는 분이 계신다
아이야, 염려하지 말자
염려 없는 우리의 맑은 노래를
새해 달력 열두 장에 그리어 두자

누가 나를 위해 울고 있는가
긴 밤을 새워 흐느끼는 소리
내 잘못은 붉은 가슴 새겨 두게 하시고
이웃의 눈물에 보답하게 하소서

# If We Are Able To Love

We'll be able to love the next year also.
Bowing our heads with hairs like the spring grass,
Cleansing our thoughts by ringing of the ancient bell,
We'll be able to make a promise to the brightest star.
If we are able to love each other,
It'll be great with us new year also.

Children, flying kites at the harvested field in village,
Children, wishing to fly in the air like a bird,
Children, shouting for joy, 'fly me, fly me high',
Dear my child, where are you going to fly?
You'll grow up tall as much as you are newly toddling.
There is one letting the words fulfilled on you as learnt.
Dear my child, let's worry not.
Let our pure songs of no worry drawn
On the twelve months in the new year calendar.

Who is crying for me?
Sobbing sounds through the night.
My faults be inscribed in my crimson heart.
Let me repay for the tears of my neighbors.

부질없는 시샘으로 원수지는 일 없고
남의 기쁨 온 맘으로 축하하게 하소서

우리들의 어린것들이 바로 가게 하시고
나는 한자리에 기다리게 하소서
젖은 손 젖은 발로 땀 흘리게 하시고
꿈을 허황되이 두지 말게 하소서
내 몫은 조금씩 모자라도 좋습니다

날마다 감사하게
그리하여 갈수록 겸허하게 하소서
다 듣고 응답하시는 분 만나고 싶은
크고 빛난 소원 하나 간직하고 싶습니다

Let me make no enemy out of the useless envy,
But let us congratulate their delights with all my heart.

Let our children walk on the right way,
But, me wait always at one place.
Let me sweat with my hands and feet wetted,
And keep myself out of a hollow dream.
I'm gratified with my lesser portions.

Let me be grateful to all every day,
So, become humbler as the time goes by.
One wish to meet him who listens and answers to me,
Such a big and splendid wish, I hope to conceive in me.

## 경청하소서

하루를 탈 없이
건넜습니다

안 풀리는 매듭은
베고 잡니다

오늘 밤 꿈속 밝힐
불꽃 같은 눈

내일 아침 돋는 해여
나를 경청하소서

# May You Listen Close To Me

Without a trouble
I've come across over a day.

I'm sleeping with my head
On the knot left entangled.

The eyes like a flame of fire,
Which will brighten my dream tonight.

The sun to rise tomorrow morn,
Please, you listen close to me.

| 이향아 영역 시집 |

# 저녁 강가에서
## By The Riverside At Eventide

**초판 발행일** 2020년 7월 10일

**지은이** 이향아
**옮긴이** 이정호
**펴낸이** 임만호
**펴낸곳** 창조문예사
**등 록** 제16-2770호(2002. 7. 23)
**주 소** 서울 강남구 선릉로112길 36(삼성동) 창조빌딩 3F(우 : 06097)
**전 화** 02) 544-3468~9
**F A X** 02) 511-3920
**E-mail** holybooks@naver.com

**책임편집** 장민혜
**디자인** 이선애
**제 작** 임성암
**관 리** 양영주

**ISBN** 979-11-86545-85-0  03810
**정 가** 15,000원

※ 잘못된 책은 바꾸어 드립니다.

By The Riverside At Eventide
Copyright©2020 by HyangAh Lee
All rights reserved. Changjomunyesa.
36, Seolleung-ro 112-gil, Gangnamgu, Seoul, Korea.

Price $15.00